A SPIRIT DAUGHTER
WORKBOOK

---

written by
Jill Wintersteen

FOR THE PISCES SEASON
February 18th - March 18th

+

THE NEW MOON
Sunday, February 23rd
7:32AM PST

PISCES

Are you ready to feel your most expansive self? Pisces is often depicted as the fish, but in reality, she is in the entire ocean, boundless, all-encompassing, and connected to everything. Pisces reminds us that we, too, are energetically connected to all vibrations in the Universe. Just as the ocean touches two shores, bridging them together, our energy connects everything around us, merging all frequencies into one. Pisces teaches us that we are the Universe, and the Universe is us. There is no distinction in the land of Pisces. Everything we desire is already ours because we embody its vibrations. We are connected through the realm of energy to our dreams and they to us. There is no need to chase our desires or even entertain the thought that we may not obtain something. Everything we can think of, and even things beyond our imagination, already exist in our infinite energetic field. All we have to do is tune into their frequency, believe in their existence in our lives, and connect to their vibration in a way that manifests them into our current reality.

Part of tuning into the frequency of our dreams is first healing parts of ourselves, which prevent us from fully connecting with them. Pisces Season is a time to heal. Pisces opens up our emotions and helps us reprocess them, making healing more accessible than other times of the year. Pisces, like all of the water signs, heightens our feelings and brings them to the surface for deeper understanding. Pisces also illuminates what emotions may not be ours, but rather another's we are connecting to in our energy. Often, the emotions we experience on a conscious and subconscious level, belong to someone else. We have absorbed them into our field unknowingly and assume they are ours, but they belong elsewhere.

Part of the work of Pisces Season is understanding which emotions are yours and which ones you have taken on from outside sources. Once you identify an emotion as not your own, take steps to acknowledge it and speak to it. Let the emotion know you see it, but also realize that it is not yours, then release it back to the Universe. For the emotions that are your own, spend some time working with them this Season. Feel into them and watch them but do not allow them to take over your conscious experience.

Pisces is the quiet observer of the zodiac. She teaches how to see your emotions as things happening rather than something happening to you. If Buddhism were represented by an astrological sign, it would be Pisces. Her energy teaches the art of observation and how it leads to a more fulfilling life devoid of emotional reactions and triggers. Pisces Season is a time to meditate daily, even for a few moments, and become the witness of your world. Resist the urge to react to your emotions or other events in your life. This process, of course, is no easy feat. We are programmed to react to our emotions, but the path of healing involves understanding your feelings and taking control of them, versus them controlling you.

As you make your way through Pisces Season, acknowledge your feelings, lean into them, breathe into them, but try not to react to them. Instead of allowing them to take over your consciousness, choose something else. Consciously choose to feel a different vibration in your energy. After all, you are connected to all vibrations, according to Pisces. If you feel unwanted feelings coming up for attention, acknowledge their existence, but choose to feel something else. Choose to feel a vibration that is under your control instead of reacting to what is not.

As you align with the non-reactive energy of Pisces, it becomes easier to trust the process and surrender to the flow of your life. We often set intentions, and then instead of patiently awaiting their fruition, we try to control each step of their manifestation. We try to force things instead of trusting the natural course of action for our dreams. We forget to hold the vision and end up micromanaging each step. Pisces reminds us that we don't always know, or understand, each step of our journey. Events may occur which seem unrelated to the progress of our dreams but are part of their evolution. Remember, according to Pisces, everything is connected. Every event, every person, and every energy is connected to your dreams. During Pisces Season, practice detached awareness with your dreams. Hold the vision of the reality you want to live, but try not to control the process. Trust that everything is unfolding exactly as it should and surrender to the ultimate flow of your life. Remember that everything is connected, and you are connected to the Universe. Your visions are already yours; all you need to do is hold space for them to become your current reality.

MOONSCOPES

Moonscopes are based on your Moon Sign. They provide guidance and insight about how your personal Moon, otherwise known as your emotions, will be affected by the Seasonal energy of Pisces. These energies will amplify on her New Moon.

Aries Moon: You are a natural doer and love a challenge. You tend to "make things happen" in your world and have never been one to sit and wait patiently. You also can be quite reactive to your emotions, as you are full of fire and passion. Over Pisces Season, challenge yourself to become the observer of your emotions. Instead of reacting to your feelings, or giving in to your impulses, try counting to ten as you breathe. Practice observing your feelings and be open to revelations that come up when you do not react in the moment. On the New Moon, envision a version of yourself who leaves space for the process to unfold instead of creating each step along the way.

Taurus Moon: You love security and stability. This Season asks you to step outside of your comfort zones and trust. You may not always know the answers, and you may not always know where the road before you will lead. Your job this Season is to find comfort in the unknowing. Challenge yourself to surrender to the notion that all will work out exactly as it is supposed to for your journey. This way of living may not feel secure, but it will open doors for you that would otherwise be closed. Surrender to your journey and watch it unfold in front of you this Season. On the New Moon, envision a version of yourself who feels secure in holding the vision of your dreams and doesn't need outside reassurance they will happen. Your inner knowing is the only assurance you need.

Gemini Moon: Your mind, and your emotions, move quickly. This fast-paced nature of your energy makes it easy for you to react to it, often without a pause. You often have so many emotions flying around at once; it becomes challenging to know which ones you are responding to at any given moment. During Pisces Season, give yourself, and your feelings, space. Take deep breaths and long pauses before reacting to any energy. In this space, become the observer and student of your energy. Understand yourself on a deeper level and ask what your emotions are teaching you in the moment. On the New Moon, envision a version of yourself who remains calm in the sea of your emotions. See yourself as the observer and in full control of every energy in your being.

Cancer Moon: You are a water sign like Pisces and will experience your emotions very intensely during this Season. Challenge yourself to learn from them without allowing them to control you. Instead, sit with them long enough that they open the door to your intuition. Pisces controls our psychic centers. Be receptive to visions coming your way. Know that the more you can become the observer of your energy, the more information will come effortlessly into your field. Answers will begin to appear, and your inner knowing will shine through any emotional turmoil. On the New Moon, envision a version of yourself who remains in control of their emotions, while still being receptive to their intuition.

Leo Moon: You are on a journey to understand compassion and unconditional love of yourself and others. Make these energies and vibrations your highest priority during Pisces Season. You have a huge heart, and when you allow it to lead the way, you attract great things into your life. During Pisces Season, hold the vision of love and compassion in your vibration. Let everything else fall into place around it. Resist the urge to control any outcome or react to others. Instead, find ways to forgive yourself for any regrets, find compassion for your journey, and love yourself unconditionally. On the New Moon, envision a version of yourself who lives in the highest vibration of love all the time. See how this frequency connects you to your highest visions.

Virgo Moon: You stand opposite of Pisces in the sky and on the zodiac wheel. Unlike Pisces, you like structure and boundaries. You need them to keep your emotions organized and to understand your feelings. During Pisces Season, challenge yourself to give in to the chaos of your emotions without reacting to them. Just allow them to be, and instead of controlling them in some way, observe them for what they are: messy, unclear, and even overwhelming. Find healing in observing the full range of your emotions. Notice what comes up to the surface when you resist controlling your feelings and instead just allow them. On the New Moon, lean into your intuition as it will be heightened. Allow it to show the way to your healing and the next steps on your path.

*You can look up your Moon Sign at astro-charts.com

MOONSCOPES

Libra Moon: You are on a quest this lifetime to find balance in your mind and energy. You fully understand that to achieve equanimity in your partnerships, you must first understand what that means on an individual level. Align with the energy of Pisces to become the observer of your mind and emotions. Allow this observation to help you achieve inner peace throughout the Season and New Moon. Observe your emotions, your natural reactions to them, and how you create calmness in your energy. Work with this first within yourself, then extend it to your partnerships, observing and learning from them. On the New Moon, envision a version of yourself who can create inner peace no matter what storm arises.

Scorpio Moon: Finally, a season which understands the importance of intuition and magic. As a fellow Water Moon, you understand Pisces and her New Moon deeply. You feel intensely and love to examine the depths of consciousness itself. One of your favorite pastimes is unraveling the inner workings of your own mind and the mind of others. Take this further with the help of Pisces and feel your consciousness merging with those around you. Feel into the oneness of everything and expand into a new understanding of the Universe. On the New Moon, see how all of your experiences are part of the larger picture of your energetic evolution. Form a new way of feeling about things, which includes this knowledge, and helps to heal you on the deepest level.

Sagittarius Moon: You tend to look outwardly for answers. You love new experiences and new perspectives. Align with Pisces this Season to look inward for new experiences right inside your own mind. Travel to the depths of your own energy and seek answers from yourself instead of others. Become fascinated this season with your imagination and where it can take you. Spend time daydreaming, writing stories in your mind, and allowing yourself to feel. Watch the inner workings of your mind as if you were watching a movie. Allow it to show you your highest visions and the path to create them. On the New Moon, spend time with yourself and your imagination, allowing it to wander to the edges of your consciousness.

Capricorn Moon: You, as an Earth Moon, tend to like definition and order. You like compartments, containers and feel reassured when everyone is in their place. In Pisces Season, there are no neatly organized boxes. There are messy emotions, with blurred lines, and blended labels. Use this time to step outside of your comfort zone and embrace chaos. Lean into your strong center, to stabilize you, as you ride the waves of this Season and embrace its all-encompassing nature. On the New Moon, craft intentions which lack specificity. Be open with your asks from the Universe and practice the art of surrender.

Aquarius Moon: You are neither emotional or reactive. You, if anything, tend to overthink, especially when it involves feelings. Align with Pisces Season to step outside of yourself and observe your energy in the moment. See your frequency and what it is attracting and what you are emitting back into the world. There is no need to analyze it, instead, challenge yourself to feel this season. Feel into your vibration and feel into the emotions which comprise it. Notice that when you allow yourself to feel, you also open up the gateway to your intuitive knowing. It becomes easier to make decisions and receive information rather than searching for it. On the New Moon, envision a version of yourself that allows emotions to unfold without getting swept away by them. Define the frequency you want to follow by observing these emotions, not suppressing them.

Pisces Moon: You are home this Season and New Moon- enjoy it! The vibrations all season will feel good to you; lean into them and develop them even further in your own being. Surrender to the process of your life. Trust that every energy is showing up at the exact moment it needs to for your evolution. Expand your consciousness even further by understanding that when you take on other's emotions, you can easily send them right back to the Universe. You are a natural healer once you understand how to release energies that are not yours. Practice releasing energies over this season by recognizing what emotions are not your own and sending them back into the universal field. On the New Moon, envision the next version of yourself who fully embraces a higher consciousness and is led only by their intuition.

*You can look up your Moon Sign at astro-charts.com

CRYSTALS FOR PISCES

Angelite is known for its power to connect us with spiritual knowledge and higher powers, like angels. It raises our awareness and allows us to connect with the universal energy and divine powers that lie within us. It also helps protect the wearer psychically by shielding the physical and energetic body from its environment. Have a piece with you when meditating or when trying to connect with your higher guidance and intuition. Angelite is blue in color.

Angelite vibrates to the Mantra: I am connected.

Labradorite is a stone of magic and healing. It helps us access our own innate magical powers. Labradorite's real power lies in its ability to help us transform our intuition into intellect to make practical decisions. It allows us to enter the void of the ethers where everything and nothing exists. From there, we can pull guiding knowledge for our journey. Have it around when you need to make a decision and need guidance from yourself and the Universe. Labradorite is grey/blue iridescent in color.

Labradorite vibrates to the mantra: I am magic.

Amethyst is the stone of dreamers. It helps us access our dreams, remember our dreams, and get lost in them. It is connected with our crown chakra and can assist in opening it to help us connect with our highest spiritual self. Amethyst is a great stone to have near you when meditating. It can calm the mind and spirit, providing a clear channel for intuition to flood in. Try placing one near your bed to help remember your dreams and to help bring in messages while you sleep. Amethyst is purple in color.

Amethyst vibrates to the mantra: I am a dreamer.

Ocean Jasper is a wonderful stone for elevating your consciousness. It helps us feel into the interconnectedness of the universe and aligns us with the frequency of the ocean. Ocean Jasper soothes our soul and reminds us that we are part of the vast Universe and all of its gifts. It is also deeply therapeutic, helping to restore energy. Ocean Jasper is a healing stone as it finds the hidden meaning in our past and integrates it with our future. Ocean Jasper is a mix of grey, yellow, and brick coloring.

Ocean Jasper vibrates to the mantra: I am elevated.

Botswana Agate is a comforting stone and helps remind us that no matter how dark our world may become, there still is light to be found. It helps align us with our inner strength and determined resolve, making it a great stone to have when giving up addictions of all kinds. Botswana Agate is also a stone of protection, shielding the wearer from psychic attacks of both living beings and spirits. Have some around your home to protect your sanctuary. Botswana Agate is pink, cream and grey in color.

Botswana Agate vibrates to the mantra: I am light.

PISCES MEDITATION

Pisces is the most spiritual sign of the zodiac, and her energy reminds us that we are spiritual beings in a human form. This Season and New Moon is one to practice our most observant self, our witness self. It is a time to watch sensations within, letting them pass instead of reacting to them. This non-reaction is the heart of mindfulness meditation, which starts by observing the feelings that exist in each area of the body. Through placing our awareness methodically on each part of our body, we are holding space for sensations, and emotions, to be felt, seen, and released. The purpose of this meditation is to train our conscious and subconscious mind to not react to events internally or externally, but merely observe them. True observation is an art form and one that needs time, commitment, and understanding. The following meditation will provide a foundation for this type of awareness. Practice this meditation every day during Pisces Season and on the New Moon. You can start with 15 minutes and increase your duration to 22 and 30 minutes as you feel comfortable.

Be Open

Before you begin the body awareness meditation, open yourself to the energies of the Universe. Either in a seated or lying down position, face your palms upward in a receptive posture. Say to yourself, "I am open to love and beauty. I am open to wealth and abundance. I am open to guidance and intuition. I am open to inspiration and my imagination." You can change these phrases to whatever suits you best, but the idea is to open yourself to receive these energies which are always available to you.

Body Awareness - 15mins

Throughout this practice, place all of your attention on one area of the body. Become completely immersed in the sensations that arise in that area of focus. When focused on an area, pay no attention to the rest of the body. Let all other sensations fade into the background, including your thoughts. As you focus on different places, feel all the sensations of that area. This can be tingling, heat, coolness, pain; you may even feel emotions. As you explore each sensation, you allow it to release. If you feel nothing at all, this is ok too. Just keep your awareness on the area, and if thoughts or feelings arise, let them pass like the rest of the sensations. Give them no attention, not even to block them. Just let them go.

Lie in a comfortable position, relaxing your entire body. Feel the ground beneath you, supporting you in every way. Release any tension from your neck, shoulders, and face. Take three deep breaths, exhaling from your mouth. With each exhale, relax even more. Allow your breathing to return to normal. Place all of your attention on the crown of the head. Spend a few breaths here, observing what arises in this area. Be genuinely curious about what may be residing here. Watch the sensations, as if you are watching a movie. If it helps to keep your concentration, you can try labeling the sensations as if you are filing them away. Resist the natural tendency to judge or evaluate these sensations. There are no good or bad feelings here, only what is happening in the present moment.

Continue moving through your body, placing your attention in different areas. Move from the head to the face, neck, shoulders, arms, hands, torso, pelvis, legs, and feet. Cover your entire body piece by piece with your attention. Spend only a few breaths on each area, not dwelling on the sensations, but giving them a chance to pass. As you give your body and energy attention, it will be able to release. Letting go is, first, a process of awareness. We need to become aware of what we are releasing before we can truly let it go from our energy. This meditation will help sharpen your attention while limiting your reactivity. If we react to sensations, they are more likely to stay. It is through conscious acknowledgment, without reaction, that the sensations pass.

As we train our mind with this meditation, we also teach ourselves how not to react in situations outside our body. We extend the practice and become observers of our emotions rather than letting our emotions control us. We eventually learn to not hold onto any energy and understand that everything is temporary.

PISCES LUNAR FLOW

The following sequence is a Yin Yoga sequence. Yin Yoga connects us with our receptive and intuitive nature, which is more concerned with restoration than alignment. Yin Yoga also differs from Yang Yoga in the length of time the poses are held. Typically we only hold poses for 30-45 seconds, which stretches the muscles. In Yin Yoga, we hold the poses from 3-5 minutes, giving freedom to the muscles and the connective tissue that holds them. Through stretching the connective tissue, we are providing space to the deeper layers of our body. If you find your mind wanders as you are holding, simply count the breath. Count up to five on each inhale and back down from five on each exhale. Before you begin, set the room up with candles, relaxing music, and anything else that soothes your soul.

Baddha Konasana // Cobbler's Pose - 5 mins
Begin in a seated position. Place the soles of your feet together, knees out to either side. If you are very tight in your hips or hamstrings, place a folded blanket underneath you. Take a deep inhale, then on exhale fold forward. Do not force anything; just allow yourself to fold into the pose. Your back can gently round and allow your head to hang completely. Breathe here for 5 minutes. As you do so, gently massage your feet. Pisces is connected to our feet and immune system, so give them some love while you are holding this pose.

Janu Sirsasana // Forward Fold - 3 mins each side
Again, if your hamstrings are tight, please sit on a folded blanket. Extend one leg out in front of you. Bend the other leg and place the foot on the inside of the opposite leg's inner thigh, allow the knee to fall out to the side. Take a deep inhale, on exhale fold forward over the extended leg. Relax into this pose, allowing the back to round and the head to relax. Breathe deeply here for 3 minutes, then slowly come out of it, switching sides.

PISCES LUNAR FLOW

Parsva Upavista Konasana Side Bend // Wide Legged Side Bend - 3 mins each side

Still on a folded blanket, bring your legs out to either side once again. Inhale reach your right arm up to the ceiling then on exhale, take it to the inside of the right leg. Revolve your chest forward and reach the other arm in line with your ear for a side stretch. On each inhale reach through both arms a bit more extending out of the waist. On exhale, turn your chest forward and towards the ceiling. When finished, slowly release, coming tor center for a few breaths then switching sides.

Upavista Konasana // Wide-Legged Forward Fold - 5 mins

Sit on a folded blanket for this one, even if your legs are flexible. Extend both of your legs and take them as wide as they will comfortably go. Inhale, and on Exhale fold forward between your legs, feeling your hips tilt forward as you fold. Relax through your entire upper body and breathe here for 5 minutes. When you are finished, slowly lift from this pose and help your legs back together.

Paschimottanasana // Seated Forward Bend

Still on the blanket, extend both of your legs out in front of you. Flex your feet to straighten your legs and activate the back of them entirely. Inhale reach your arms up overhead, exhale fold forward over your legs. Allow your arms and hands to land wherever it is comfortable. Relax through your legs and your neck. You may place a block in between your legs to rest your forehead upon if this is comfortable for you. Hold here for 5 mins, breathing deeply into your back body, allowing it release. Afterward, slowly come out of it, returning to an upright position. Hold here, neutralizing your spine for a moment.

Viparita Karani //Legs Up the Wall Pose 5-10 mins.

You will need to be near a wall for this pose. Grab a bolster or a folded blanket and lay down near a wall. Scoot your butt as close to the wall as possible and place the blanket underneath you. Then swing your legs up the wall. You may have to inch in a little closer, just make sure it feels comfortable and supported. Your legs should be able to completely relax as if they are suspended in the air. Once you're comfortable, relax your arms and have your palms facing up in a receptive position. Close your eyes and relax here for 5-10 minutes. When you've finished, slowly take your legs down and relax on one side for a moment before returning to seated.

Supported Matsyasana // Fish Pose - 5 mins

Take your bolster or rolled up blanket back to the middle of the room. Set it up lengthwise and lie on it so it runs down the length of your back. As you lay on it, feel your chest open, and your heart expands. Stretch your arms out to either side with your palms facing upwards. Your legs can either be straight or bent in a baddha konasana shape. Lie here for 5 minutes. Feel yourself receiving the gifts of the universe and practice the art of being.

Savasana - 5 minutes

Slowly roll off your bolster, pausing to one side. Remove the bolster and return to your back, now flat on the ground. Stretch your legs out long on the mat, you may place the bolster under your knees to release tension from your lower back. Have your palms facing upward in a receptive motion. Allow your entire weight to be supported by the floor beneath you as you rest. Let go of the counting of the breath and breathe naturally, observing the quiet flow of each inhale and exhale.

ALIGNING the SPIRIT

Tips for Going with the Flow

> The magic is not in the fixed road -
> it's in the flow.
>
> - spirit daughter

Become aware of your methods of control.

The first step to going with the flow is releasing control. To let go of the reins a bit, you must first become aware of how you control things in the first place. We all have our different methods; it's time to figure out yours. Once you build this awareness, it will be easier to spot the times when you go into these automatic control patterns and adjust them. Some common methods of control are: over-scheduling followed by inflexibility with your time, planning out every detail, leaving no room for serendipity, positioning yourself as an authority so others will follow your lead, and not including other people's opinions in your plans. There are some instances, of course, where these methods are a good thing and needed, but there are also times when they become blocks to receiving magic. Learn to recognize when control is necessary and when you can be more flexible in your energy.

Get comfortable with being uncomfortable.

Going with the flow can take us out of our comfort zone. It is challenging to release control and surrender to the universe. We, by nature, are planners and doers. Going with the flow requires us to be spontaneous, to shift unexpectedly, and receive rather than do. For most of us, this is not our natural state and can bring up feelings of anxiety and worry. It can make us feel uncomfortable in our own skin. If we can learn to step back from these feelings and observe them rather than react to them through control, we are one step closer to going with the flow. We need to become comfortable, or at least accepting, of feeling uncomfortable at times. The more we practice just observing, rather than reacting to the sensations which arise when we are not in control, the more they will pass or at least start to feel normal and non- threatening.

Release expectations.

Expectations are a primary barrier to going with the flow. When we have expectations, we subconsciously seek to control the energies around us to meet them. No one wants disappointment because of unmet expectations. Most of the time, we don't even know we have expectations until we are let down because what we wanted was not delivered. In any situation, first become aware of what expectations you are bringing with you. These expectations can be for yourself and also for others. We can have expectations for our environment itself, for example, expecting the weather to be sunny and beautiful, only to be met with clouds and rain. Once you've become aware of your expectations, try to release them. Be open to any and all possibilities, knowing you will be handed exactly what you need when you need it. When you enter into any situation or relationship, without expectations, you leave room for freedom, growth, and the unimaginable.

Embrace new lessons and opportunities to learn.
Whenever we let go of control and go with the flow, we run the risk of things not going as planned- that's part of the point and the adventure! Attempt to see everything which comes your way as an opportunity to learn. This even includes seemingly mistakes, mishaps, and disappointments. They are all lessons in disguise. When we let go of control, we open the door for learning and integrations of new energies. Practice shifting your perception to see every event, person, and moment as a new piece of information in this ever-evolving world you live.

Recognize "you" don't always know what is best.
Not even the smartest person in the world knows everything, so how can you expect yourself to? When we insist on controlling every piece of our life, we are telling the universe, and our higher self, that we know what is best. This cannot be the case because our conscious mind does not have all the information. Most of us do not have access to the future, or even to our greater life plan. When we surrender control, we are giving the universe permission to take over some of the decision making for us. It's important to recognize that you're really giving control over to your life's journey and your higher self. This is the part of us that does know everything because it is connected to universal knowledge. As you accept that you do not know everything all the time, it becomes easier to surrender to the flow of your life.

Trust.
Trust is like a muscle; the more we use it, the stronger it becomes. At first, it can be hard to surrender and trust the flow of your life. Most of us don't even know what that looks like, or how to know if we are doing it. The more you stop controlling, the easier it will be to spot signs, signals, and coincidences which bring you into the natural rhythm of your life. As you let go of control of every detail, you'll start running into the right people who can help you, seeing the right messages in your inbox, and you'll even start noticing the foods you need to incorporate to feel your best self. The "right" energies will begin appearing more vibrant. When you are faced with two options, one will seem more attractive. Imagine you are in the forest, and two paths present themselves. When we are in the flow, not overthinking, and in a state of trust, the "right" path for us will seem more vibrant, more energized, and will FEEL good to our soul. Our brain will likely want to weigh every outcome, but when we release the need to control, we can clearly "see" the right path for us. In comes trust. You take the leap, you follow the well-lit path, you speak to the person you've seen three times "randomly" this week. The more you trust, the more signs you'll receive, the more signs you follow, the more reinforcement you'll have to trust. And the cycle continues infinitely.

NEW MOON

FEBRUARY 23RD

PISCES IN...	FOCUS ON...
1ST HOUSE	Focus on observing how you present your identity to the world.
2ND HOUSE	Focus on observing how you connect with self-worth and abundance.
3RD HOUSE	Focus on observing how you communicate both overtly and subtly.
4TH HOUSE	Focus on observing how you define your home.
5TH HOUSE	Focus on observing your relationship with joy.
6TH HOUSE	Focus on observing how you feel when of service to others.
7TH HOUSE	Focus on observing how you interact with your partners.
8TH HOUSE	Focus on observing how respond to energies which encourage personal growth.
9TH HOUSE	Focus on observing how you integrate new knowledge and truths.
10TH HOUSE	Focus on observing how you balance work and self-care.
11TH HOUSE	Focus on observing how you feel when part of a larger collective.
12TH HOUSE	Focus on defining your spiritual path and growth.

NEW MOON

FEBRUARY 23RD

The New Moon is one of the most powerful times of the lunar cycle. The Moon's energy is subtle at this time, cloaked in darkness, but still immense in its ability to create dramatic shifts in our vibration. New Moons occur every month when the Moon meets the Sun in our skies. They represent the start of a new Lunar Cycle, ripe with potential and possibility. As the Moon and Sun meet, so do their very oppositional energies. The meeting of both day and night creates a force that we can harness to make changes in our lives. As these otherwise opposing cosmic forces meet, they create a spark in the cosmos, which becomes the seed for new beginnings and new frequencies to evolve through the Lunar Cycle. This spark is what makes our intentions set on a New Moon so potent. Each month, we have the chance to begin again. We can choose what vibrations we are calling into our world. When we consciously choose which energies we want to embody, we empower ourselves to manifest any dream. We tell the Universe what we are ready to receive and what we are welcoming into our lives. These messages are heard most clearly on the New Moon, making it the perfect time to define our lives.

The magic of the New Moon comes from the meeting of the Sun and the Moon. During a New Moon, these opposing forces come together. We act as a reflection of these energies, and opposing forces within us merge to form a unified whole, capable of transmitting our highest intentions. The Sun and Moon conjunction reminds us that even seemingly opposing forces in nature are still similar in their core energy. The Sun is Yang energy. He is masculine in nature, action-oriented, warm, and motivates us to DO. The Moon is Yin energy. She is feminine, intuitive, receptive, and cooling. The Moon motivates us to BE.

We, too, have both Yin and Yang energies within us. No matter your gender, your vibration holds the frequency of both feminine and masculine energy. These energies can work in harmony, like a good marriage, or they can pull each other in opposite directions. The key is balance. We must always find ways to bring our energy back to balance, whether it means nurturing our Yin or nurturing our Yang. The end goal is the same; full integration of all energies.

The New Moon affords us a time to bring balance to our entire system, body, mind, and spirit. Through the unification of Moon and Sun, Yin and Yang, every New Moon, we have the opportunity to create equanimity in our energy. We can feel areas that are off-balance and decide what we need to bring them into harmony. Are there places where you could embody the energy of Moon more? How can you receive answers instead of creating them? Likewise, are there places you can embody the energy of the Sun more? Where could you have more motivation or more action in your life? A great question to ask every New Moon is: Am I "being" as much as I'm "doing" and vice versa? This simple question can hold the keys to helping restore balance in your vibration and your life.

Every New Moon is positioned in a zodiac sign. This month, we have the New Moon in Pisces, where the Sun is located for four weeks. Pisces themes our New Moon and helps us focus our energy. We can harness the power of Pisces to find imbalances in our energy and utilize her vibration to restore equanimity in our system. A great place to start working with the New Moon energy is the astrological house ruled by Pisces in your chart. You can look up your houses up at astro-charts.com. Here you will find your zodiac wheel. Look to the outside of the wheel for Pisces, and then look to the inside wheel for the corresponding house number. Houses represent areas of your life. If, for instance, your eighth house is ruled by Pisces, then this New Moon will affect that area to your life to a greater degree and may even illuminate imbalances in your Yin and Yang energy here. The chart on the opposite page gives you an idea of where to focus your energy this New Moon depending on which house is ruled by Pisces. You can always focus your intentions on any area of your life which calls to you, but if you need help in choosing which piece to focus on, look to your houses for guidance.

The overall key to any New Moon is balance. When the two most powerful astrological bodies in our immediate cosmos come together and balance their energy, it's an opportunity for us to follow along. Each New Moon allows us to create harmony in our system, and from the harmony, we can clearly feel and see our highest visions. Our intuition speaks more loudly, and we can receive the answers we seek while understanding what to do with them.

PISCES X NEW MOON

When the New Moon meets Pisces, magic is in the air. This is a Moon to receive. It is not one of action but one of simple presence. The combination of the Yin energy of the Moon and the vibration of Pisces, opens up all of our psychic centers, allowing us to tap into our infinite connection to universal energy. When we open ourselves to the full frequency of the Universe, we feel supported, loved, and capable of manifesting any dream. There is always a free-flowing energy of positivity in the world that is available to all of us. Our job is to break down the blocks which prevent these vibrations from entering our field. The Universe wants to help make our dreams come true because we are the Universe. When we say the Universe supports us, what we are referring to is our highest self coming through to guide our every intention. Pisces teaches us there is no distinction between us and every other energy. On this New Moon, embrace the full meaning of your all-encompassing energy and open your consciousness to connecting with the positive vibrations which exist around and within you each day.

We often feel we need to do something on the New Moon to harness its power. While writing intentions and expressing your dreams is always a positive practice, this a Moon to simply BE. Often doing nothing is the hardest thing we can ever "do." Sitting with yourself in the silence of your own energy can feel very challenging if you are a natural doer. Embrace the notion, this New Moon, that by doing nothing, you are doing everything. Spend time in meditation, connect with nature, allow your mind to wander from daydream to daydream. It is in this space of nothingness that you can hear the guidance of the Universe. The quieter you become, the easier it is to connect with your intuition. Answers pop up in the form of visions, and you will instantly know what next steps are needed to manifest your dreams. No effort is required, only the effort to sit uninterrupted by the world around you.

As you sit with yourself, surrender to the guidance of the Universe and trust the process. Know that there may be things you cannot control in your world and even things you cannot influence. Give permission to the Universe to help you in areas that you need support and trust that you will receive exactly what you need when you need it. Reflect on times in your life where you were fully supported, and trust that support is available to you every moment of every day. Furthermore, the wisdom of the Universe is always available to you. You are connected to more knowledge than you could ever imagine. It is through quiet contemplation that this knowledge becomes available to you once you open yourself to receiving it. On this New Moon declare to the Universe that you are open to receiving support, you are open to receiving love and beauty, and you are open to receiving guidance and intuition. Then cultivate patience and trust. Throughout the day, be aware of your thoughts and your imagination. Watch the images and ideas which spontaneously come into your mind. Do not dismiss any of them; pay attention to each thought, hunch, and a-ha moment. Observe your mind and energy and know that the Universe is always speaking through you.

Throughout this New Moon, allow your mind to settle and explore the infinite space outside of yourself. Surrender to your imagination and embrace the visions it shows you. This is an excellent Moon to free form draw or paint. You can even write poetry with no agenda in mind. Find ways to express what you are receiving and give some form to the energy of the day. The key to working with this New Moon's energy is detaching from any goals or expectations. This Moon may bring you new insights, but it may also just provide a space for you to explore your own energy. It may be a time of restoration and healing for you, or it may be a time of creativity when new methods of expression surface in your consciousness. Be open to all of it without expecting any of it. Make a commitment to be fully present with yourself this New Moon. Be receptive to the energy of the day, and without reacting to it, allow it into your vibration, bringing you knowledge and guidance in any form available. Most importantly, remember to have compassion for yourself this Moon as you learn about your most subtle layers. You are a part of the infinite Universe, but you are also a human learning about yourself and how to live in an energetic world. Hold space for your continued evolution and keep returning to the vibration of love, which is always available to you.

Aspects

This New Moon is conjunct Mercury Retrograde in Pisces. Mercury Retrograde turns our communication inward, a wonderful addition to this New Moon. It allows us to explore the inner workings of our energy on a deeper level and can help us reprocess old events. Mercury Retrograde's energy on this New Moon can provide profound healing as we reflect on past pain and trauma and find new ways to understand it in our energy. We can have a different conversation with ourself about the same emotion and, in that reprocessing, change our perspective. As you move through this New Moon, be open to receiving guidance on new ways to understand old emotions and feelings. Also, allow your imagination to show you a new way of being, continually asking yourself who you would be without a certain thought or feeling. Envision a different version of yourself, one who has different ways of communicating the same feeling. Take the time this New Moon to be open to the gifts of Mercury Retrograde and allow it to show you a new reality.

This New Moon is also sextile Uranus in Taurus and Mars in Capricorn, meaning both of these energies affect the New Moon. A sextile aspect occurs when cosmic bodies are sixty degrees apart. It is a beneficial aspect where the energies enhance one another and bring out the higher vibrations of each frequency involved. Uranus in Taurus adds new perspectives and bold visions to this New Moon. It helps enhance our imagination of what is possible for us to manifest. It also helps ground our energy with the Earth element and reminds us to connect with nature for inspiration and knowledge. Uranus' influence on this New Moon asks: What does your future self want to tell you, and how can it enhance your present?

On the other side of the sky, there is Mars in Capricorn, also forming a sextile with this New Moon. Mars in Capricorn is another grounding force and can help us connect to our passion this New Moon. This energy can compel us to act upon something, but it's important to feel into the Earth energy of this transit, instead, to help us stay centered and present. Feel into what motivates you, but resist the urge to react to it. Instead, connect with your commitment to receive information about your next steps before you take them.

stay
in
your
magic

SETTING UP for MAGIC

Each zodiac sign carries inherent energy. With this energy comes colors, shapes, scents, and elements which match its vibration. For every New Moon, we want to incorporate as many of these frequencies as possible. While none of them are required to align with the energy of the New Moon, they do help reflect the energy. Think of them as energetic mirrors placed around the room to amplify and direct the energy. Use your intuition to guide the choice and placement of objects. Resist the urge to overthink where they belong. Let the crystals, in particular, choose their location; all you need to do is listen.

Pick a space that feels centered and stable, either inside or outside. Imagine a white light creating the boundary of the circle and place candles, crystals, and other items within this boundary. Place a crystal, candle, or another piece of magic in the center to give structure to the circle. This is also where you can set up a crystal grid to help direct the energy further. If you are creating an altar, you can place it in the easterly corner to help call in the energy of new beginnings. Know that your attention and awareness of the energy available is the most important thing for working with it. You can practice the exercises in this workbook in any way you choose; you can practice alone, on a train, or in a group of people around a bonfire. Your willingness to open up, to look within, and expand your consciousness is the most essential piece to this day.

The other pieces for calling in and aligning with the energy of Pisces are listed below. You can combine them in any way you like.

Colors: Lavender, Greys, Light Purples and Grey Blues
Shapes: Waves
Texture/Fabric: Silk, Marble
Scents: Lavender, Cypress, Champaka
Flowers: Lotus, Water Lily, Lilac

As much as possible, incorporate all these elements into your circle. Use candles for Fire, a room diffuser or spray for Air, the crystals and flowers to represent Earth, and have some Water in a metal bowl. Once you set up your circle, cleanse the space with sage or palo santo. After the circle is cleansed, smudge yourself and your friends before they enter the circle.

You can begin the circle by acknowledging everyone in the room. You can then continue to the yoga if you are practicing, and then the meditation. Once you feel the room is centered, begin to talk about the astrology of the night and what it means for each of you. If it is a larger circle, you may want to designate a talking stick or crystal to give to each guest while they speak. After you've shared your understandings, continue with the questions in the workbook and the journaling portion. After everyone has finished, talk again about your experiences with the energy and the revelations which may have occurred. You can share as little or as much as you like with the group. Never feel obligated to speak; sometimes energies need time to develop before they are brought to the light of day. At this point, you may also pull some cards to help tune further into your intuitive guidance. You can use tarot cards, Goddess cards, animal medicine cards, or any other decks that may be in your toolkit.

Once you've finished the circle, close it by having everyone shut their eyes and meditate on what they are grateful for tonight and every night. You can even practice being grateful for things that haven't come your way yet. Gratitude will attract them to your energetic field and let the Universe know you are ready to receive them. Enjoy this time to be with yourself, your heart, and your soul. Get to know yourself on a deeper level and allow your life to unfold another layer each New Moon.

Lessons from Pisces:

- intuition is a superpower.

- peace comes from trusting the process.

- nothing is permanent, including your problems.

- it's possible to attract more by doing less.

- spirit daughter

NEW MOON QUESTIONS

The next pages are for you to open up to yourself and receive the answers your soul already knows. Take your time with each question and be as honest with yourself as possible. You can always return to the breath as a resting place. Answer these questions on the day or days around the New Moon. Trust the process.

1. How does it feel to just be? Are you comfortable doing nothing? What helps you sit in stillness?

_____
_____
_____
_____
_____
_____
_____
_____
_____
_____
_____
_____
_____
_____
_____
_____
_____
_____
_____
_____
_____
_____

2. In what areas of your life can you let go of control and trust the process more? What helps you feel supported in doing this?

3. In what ways does your intuition speak to you? How can you cultivate more space to hear it and your inner guidance?

_____

_____

_____

_____

_____

_____

_____

_____

_____

_____

_____

_____

_____

_____

_____

_____

_____

_____

_____

_____

_____

_____

_____

_____

4. What are your most common emotional reactions? How can you acknowledge them without reacting to them or allowing them to take over your conscious reality? How does it feel to be the witness of them?

INTENTION SETTING

Now is the time to dream and plant seeds of intent. In dreaming, we write the future of our lives by stating our desires to the Universe. It cannot give us what we don't know we want. Part of writing our intentions is to become clear in our energy for what we want to attract and manifest in our life. Intentions help guide our life, but they are flexible. It's important to plant intentions with firm commitments to them but be unattached to the outcome. Some of your intentions may come into fruition exactly as you imagined them, while others will evolve and give you something you couldn't even imagine but exactly what you need. The important part is to start the process by becoming crystal clear on what type of energy you want to feel, and you want around you, then allow the process to unfold at its own pace.

As you plant intentions, this New Moon be open to receiving visions, guidance, and help from the Universe. Be open to your intuition and adjust your intentions as needed, sometimes even days after the New Moon, when new information is revealed to you. Before beginning, state what you are open to receiving from the Universe this night. Examples are: "I am open to receiving love and beauty; I am open to receiving intuition and guidance; "I am open to receiving the lessons I need for my energy to evolve." These can be anything that supports your dreams and intentions but gives the universe space to hand you the energies you ultimately need.

Then begin to write a scene in which everything you desire is already yours. Perhaps you want a new career or a new partner. You may want a new home or a new lifestyle that incorporates more time for self-care and nourishment. Envision the next version of yourself and see a day of this person's life play out in your mind. Write down the details of this scene, including the vibrations this person carries with them and how it feels to live this life.

Afterward, create a feeling within you, which represents how you would like to feel after all of your dreams have come true. Do not worry about the dream itself at this point, just the feeling. Write down exactly how it feels to live your dream. Are you happy? Content? Grateful? Do you rise out of bed each morning with ease? If you have a partner, how does it feel to be in their company? Do not worry about how you will get there or the list of to-dos needed to accomplish your goals. Just focus on the feeling of already living your dream. Know with every ounce of your being that it is already true. It already exists for you.

On the Pisces New Moon, remember to receive your dreams and visions. Hand over some of the control to the Universe and be open to exploring what it shows you. Take your time with writing these intentions, giving yourself space to pause, reflect, and even daydream. Honor your intuition, and if you feel waiting to write these dream sequences is better for you, then continue with it another day. The key here is allowing. Allow your dreams to bubble up to the surface, not forcing them or even searching for them. Allow them to reveal themselves to you. Align with Pisces to observe your visions and your reactions to them. Often, what we receive on a Pisces New Moon is not what we expect. Write without limits and be open to the Universe, filling in some of the details. As you write, feel a sense of gratitude for what you are dreaming; thank the Universe for giving it to you and thank yourself for creating it. Gratitude always raises your vibration and creates abundance.

INTENTION SETTING

AFFIRMATIONS

Look back at the intentions and dreams you just set. Begin to notice any subtle resistance to them in your body, mind, or energy. What does that little voice inside of you say in protest to the reality you are creating. Is there any part of you that does not believe it is possible? First, make a list of any doubts, fears, or what if's that pop into your mind when reviewing your dreams. Next, make a list of statements that oppose those negative mantras. They can be the direct opposite in meaning, or they can redirect your mind to something more positive, which proves the original statement false. Create as many affirmations as you like, which support you in holding the frequency of your dream. Repeat them at the start of each day to set your vibration and help you hold your vision.

Write your old affirmations.   Write your new affirmations.

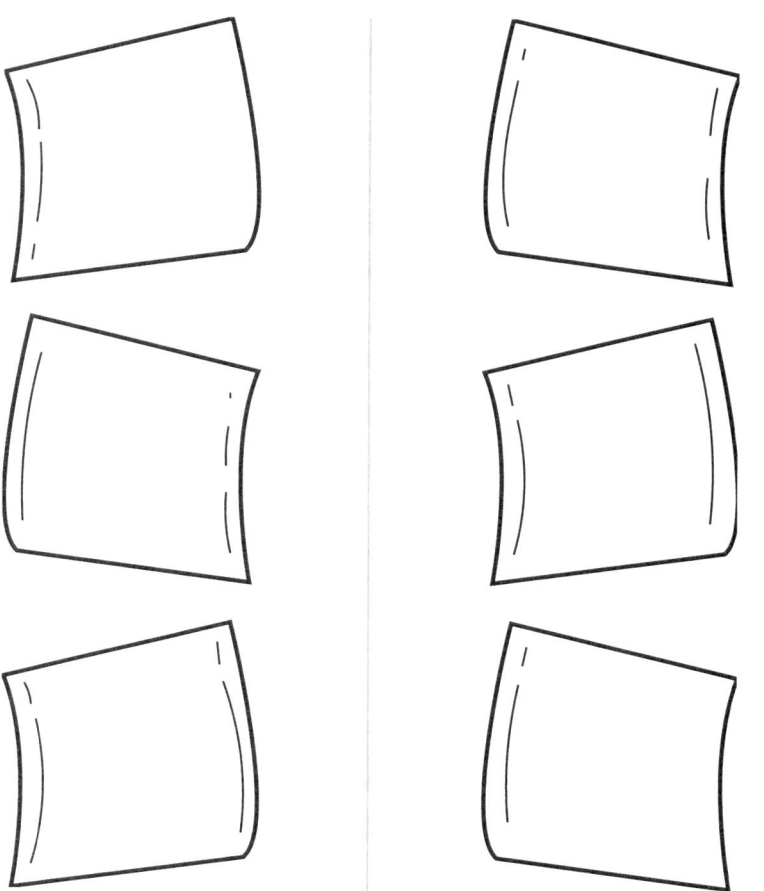

PERSONAL SIGNS

People with their Sun in Pisces tend to be the dreamers, the wanderers, and the poets of the zodiac. They love to explore the depths of their own consciousness through meditation, daydreaming, and staring into the wonders of nature. Pisces Suns feel deeply and never shy away from their emotions. They need plenty of time and space to explore their feelings to understand them. Pisces Suns benefit greatly from daily writing and journaling exercises. They need methods to express their emotions without reacting to them. Pisces Suns are on a mission this life to become the observers of their energies, always learning to take the position of the witness. They are merely the vessels for the frequencies passing through them.

Pisces Suns are also highly intuitive. They have a psychic nature about them and often "know" things before they exist in the physical realm. It may take many years for them to trust their intuition, but when they do, their life unfolds effortlessly in front of them. Pisces Suns are on a journey to trust themselves and their inner knowing. Their life path is a spiritual one, and they benefit significantly from practices like yoga and meditation. Pisces Suns need time alone with themselves and their energy to truly understand it.

PERSONAL SIGNS

Once they have mastered their internal landscape, Pisces Suns have the capacity to become great healers for others. Part of their healing ability lies in their ability to empathize with another and actually feel their pain. Through embodying another person's energy, they intuitively know what that person needs to heal. Pisces Suns become guides for others and can offer their inherent wisdom to facilitate deep healing. They do need to be cautious of taking on too much energy from another that they lose touch with themselves. Again, this is where meditation helps Pisces Suns. They need time alone to sort out what is their energy and what belongs to another. They also need practices that help them cleanse themselves of unwanted energy and return to their home frequency.

Pisces Suns must be careful of their need to escape. Often this comes from the fact that they just feel too much. They feel everything, and these energies can become overwhelming. They can feel lost in a sea of emotions, leading them to numb them out through various addictions. This includes drug or alcohol use, addiction to television, sleeping too much; it might even include addiction to certain emotions like depression, which suppresses their natural creativity. If a Pisces Sun finds themselves aligning with these low sides, it's important to find what inspires them. They must continually seek inspiration and outlets for their imagination. As they learn to express the full capacity of their energy, emotions become less overwhelming, and they can choose a higher frequency.

People with their Moon in Pisces are also sensitive to energies around them. They must learn to process their emotions wisely, and separate out what is theirs and what is other people's. They, too, are very emotional and need outlets for their feelings. Pisces Moons need to express their feelings through creative endeavors, may it be art, poetry, dancing, or singing. It's important for them to find these outlets and keep their energy flowing outward. If they fail to express their energies, then they turn inward, and depression or anxiety can take over.

Pisces Moons are also great healers. They carry ancient wisdom with them and often don't need the advice of anyone except themselves. They are highly intuitive and contain a great deal of inner knowledge. They benefit from daily meditation and time to connect with their intuition. They are often presented with many challenges to accept their psychic visions, and when they do, their life flows in a natural rhythm. When they don't follow what they know to be true, they can end up in a sea of regret and wishing they had listened to themselves all along.

Pisces Moons also need to connect with like-minded souls, or they can end up feeling alone drifting at sea. They must be wary of codependent relationships, though, and need to continually learn how to bring themselves back to their essence. Again, meditation can help with this and also the recognition of when they do lose themselves in another. If they do feel they have lost themselves, Pisces Moons need to align back with what inspires them, what makes them feel grounded, and what reminds them of their internal power. Pisces Moons carry potent energy and must always remember they can create any reality and any dream. This remembrance of their power also helps when their emotions become overwhelming. Pisces Moons always have the choice in what feeling they are experiencing; they just to need to empower themselves to choose it.

WAXING MOON

FEB 24TH - MARCH 8TH

As the Moon builds light, you are also building energy towards your dreams. In the world of energy and vibrations, like attracts like. The more you cultivate a vibration within yourself, the more of that same vibration will appear in your life. One way of manifesting your dreams is to shift your vibration to match that of your desires. During this Waxing Moon period, consciously place your attention on thoughts, emotions, and ideas which inspire a particular vibration within you. Below write down the vibration you want to cultivate more of in your life and what you will do to create this vibration in yourself first, thus attracting more of it into your world.

I WANT MORE OF THIS
VIBRATION IN MY LIFE

I WILL CREATE THAT
VIBRATION BY

WAXING MOON

FEB 24TH - MARCH 8TH

TRANSITS

MARCH 2ND: FIRST QUARTER IN GEMINI

First Quarter Moons bring us the energy of growth and action. It's a time to revisit your intentions from the New Moon and nurture them with your energy and your attention. With Gemini flavoring this Moon, it becomes a time of socialization. Gemini loves to communicate and exchange information. Talk it out this Moon. Share your dreams with others, and they may be able to help you. Through sharing your desires with others, you bring your dreams into this reality and outside of your own head. Just hearing your dreams out loud speaks them into existence. It signals to the Universe you are ready for them, and you are ready to be seen embodying them by the people around you.

This First Quarter Moon asks: Who can you share your dreams with that will support them and help you tune into your vibration?

MARCH 4TH: MERCURY RETROGRADE ENTERS AQUARIUS

Mercury Retrograde moves today from Pisces to Aquarius. In Pisces, this transit helps us access our imagination more and understand our emotions from a different perspective. In Aquarius, Mercury Retrograde compels us to question the very foundation of the way we think. Aquarius governs the mental realm and often asks us to think outside of the proverbial box by extending our consciousness to include new and different perspectives. Its influence on Mercury Retrograde can cause us to question ourselves, our way of thinking, and even or perceptions of the world around us. As Mercury moves backwards through Aquarius, ask yourself if you can embrace new ways of thinking which support the frequency you are trying to cultivate in your life.

Mercury Retrograde in Aquarius asks: How do your thoughts influence your vibration?

MARCH 4TH: VENUS ENTERS TAURUS

Venus returns to one of her astrological homes today. Venus traditionally rules Taurus, and their meeting inspires artistic endeavors and the willingness to embrace a slower-paced life full of love and beauty. With Venus in Taurus, the energy is supporting us in nourishing ourselves and grounding our energy. This energetic combination wants us to commit to the process of love, no matter who or what may be the subject. This goes for romantic love, but also for the love of ourselves, our projects, and our friends. This transit is about enjoying the details and the journey. So for the next few weeks, spend time nourishing your creativity, your love, and commitments. Slow down, enjoy life for what it is, and connect with your heart at its deepest level.

Venus in Taurus asks: What beauty do you want to create to align with the vibration of love?

MARCH 9TH: FULL MOON IN VIRGO + MERCURY TURNS DIRECT IN AQUARIUS
Please refer to the Full Moon Virgo Workbook.

WANING MOON

MARCH 10TH – MARCH 23RD

TRANSITS

MARCH 16TH: MERCURY ENTERS PISCES

Mercury, now moving direct, re-enters Pisces. Mercury, in Pisces, opens our mind and expands our imagination. It is a time of creativity when our fantasies can come to life, and we can dream up any reality. Mercury rules our communication. In Pisces, we gain access to our intuitive knowledge and visions, which may be beyond our words. This transit can help us bring form to our imagination so we can share it with the world around us, but it may be difficult at times to communicate the vastness we are experiencing in our own consciousness. Spend time in meditation to clear your thoughts and to dive deeper into your energy. Resist the urge to share what you learn about yourself until you have a firm understanding of your self-explorations. Do, however, give yourself plenty of ways to express your creativity. Write yourself daily poems, spend time journaling or just writing down a stream of consciousness, and be open to new ways to communicate your inner knowledge.

Mercury in Pisces asks:
How can you share your creativity to others in way they can understand?

MARCH 16TH: LAST QUARTER MOON IN SAGITTARIUS

Today the Sun and Moon square off bringing us our second half Moon of the Lunar Cycle in the sign of the adventurous truth seeker Sagittarius. Last Quarter Moons are a time to clear out vibrations which you do not want affecting the seeds you will plant of the next New Moon. It's also a time to decide what to keep in your energetic field and continue to nourish as you plan the next version of yourself.

Sagittarius asks us to choose our adventures based on the stories we tell ourselves. If life is a grand journey of exploration and learning, what truths do you want to carry as you walk your path? Sagittarius reminds us that the things we tell ourselves, and our beliefs in the world, attract the people and frequencies that meet us on the way. We are constantly calling in our reality based on our vibration. We are also calling in our serendipity and alignment.

The Last Quarter Moon in Sagittarius asks: What mantras are you telling yourself daily,
and how do they impact your vibration?

MARCH 19TH: ARIES SEASON BEGINS + SPRING EQUINOX

Please refer to the Aries Season and New Moon Workbook.

UP NEXT:
FULL MOON IN VIRGO
MARCH 9TH

PREPARE TO CONNECT WITH YOUR INNER GODDESS.

AVAILABLE NOW!

HAPPY NEW MOON

Thank you to everyone who supported and purchased this workbook.

Special Thanks to Rebecca Reitz (rebeccareitz.com, @becca_reitz) for her beautiful artwork on the cover, page 2, 08, 28, 33.

Thank You to Dave Mullen (@davyj0nes) for his image on page 10.

For a monthly subscription contact hello@spiritdaughter.com or visit www.spiritdaughter.com. Follow along our journey IG: @spiritdaughter

Disclaimer: The exercises and yoga sequences in this book are physical activities that should be performed carefully to avoid injury. You agree to accept all risks and release Spirit Daughter and any guest instructors from any and all liabilities. Please take care and enjoy.